God Acknowledged In What He Has Wrought, And His Continued Blessing Solicited: A Sermon

William Naylor

In the interest of creating a more extensive selection of rare historical book reprints, we have chosen to reproduce this title even though it may possibly have occasional imperfections such as missing and blurred pages, missing text, poor pictures, markings, dark backgrounds and other reproduction issues beyond our control. Because this work is culturally important, we have made it available as a part of our commitment to protecting, preserving and promoting the world's literature. Thank you for your understanding.

GOD ACKNOWLEDGED IN WHAT HE HAS WROUGHT,
AND HIS CONTINUED BLESSING SOLICITED:

A SERMON,

PREACHED AT DEPTFORD, OCTOBER 25, 1839,

ON OCCASION OF

THE CELEBRATION

OF THE

CENTENARY OF WESLEYAN METHODISM

IN THAT CIRCUIT.

TO WHICH ARE ADDED,

METRICAL MUSINGS ON CENTENARY SUBJECTS.

BY WILLIAM NAYLOR.

"The voice of rejoicing and salvation is in the tabernacles of the righteous."—DAVID.

LONDON:
PRINTED FOR THE AUTHOR,
AND SOLD BY JOHN MASON, 14, CITY-ROAD,
AND 66, PATERNOSTER-ROW.

1839.

LONDON:
PRINTED BY T. ROCHE, 70, OLD-STREET ROAD.

TO THE

MEMBERS OF THE METHODIST SOCIETIES

IN THE DEPTFORD CIRCUIT,

THIS CENTENARY SERMON

IS AFFECTIONATELY INSCRIBED,

BY THEIR PASTOR AND SUPERINTENDENT,

WITH HIS PRAYERS FOR THEIR SPIRITUAL PROSPERITY.

As the author of the following Sermon has no expectation that it will be extensively read beyond the limits of the Circuit in which it was preached, and by more than a few of his personal friends, it may be asked, why he has published statements which must be very familiar to most of his readers. His answer is,—when preached, many not united with the Methodists in church fellowship were present, and he deemed it his duty, on such a memorable occasion, briefly to bring before them what Methodism is, in its doctrines and discipline, that it might be known through what means it has attained its influence and elevation in the world; and having done so in the pulpit he did not feel himself at liberty to expunge those parts of the discourse when it was committed to the press. The Preacher, in publishing his Centenary Sermon, is actuated by the desire of recording his grateful sentiments for WESLEYAN METHODISM, to which, under God, he owes his station in life, and his hope of heavenly happiness. In his own family its blessed moral effects have been experienced by five generations, and he earnestly prays that the descendants of his sainted progenitors may continue an uninterrupted succession of faithful Methodists as long as they have a name on the earth. But should any of them ever become ashamed of, or estranged from, the spiritual family of their ancestors, he is anxious that his Sermon should remain to testify against their folly and ingratitude.

Deptford, November 6th, 1839.

A SERMON.

"Thy God hath commanded thy strength: strengthen, O God, that which thou hast wrought for us."—Psal. lxviii. 28.

There are strong reasons to warrant the conclusion that this Psalm was composed by David, and composed by him for the express purpose of being sung by the children of Israel on the very joyful occasion of removing the ark from the house of Obed-edom, to a permanent residence in mount Sion. In the ark Jehovah deigned to make his presence known, and there he frequently displayed his majesty and glory; so that what was done by it is spoken of as being done by the Lord, who is described as ascending the heights of Sion, "leading captivity captive," and taking possession of his holy residence, attended by the thousands of his angels. This interesting and triumphant procession to Sion has been considered a typical representation of the glorious ascension of the conquering Redeemer of the world from his incarnate abode on earth to his exalted throne in heaven; and to him the words of David are distinctly applied by the Holy Spirit in the New Testament. (Eph. iv. 8.)

The Psalm is principally devoted to a grateful record of the wondrous works of God, his works in the ways of his providence, and that in special reference to the Jewish nation. They had been assailed and oppressed by numerous enemies, but now those enemies were defeated and subdued, and they had become a mighty and an honourable people; for which they were exhorted to praise and bless God. And lest they should be disposed to ascribe any part of their greatness and glory to the schemes of their own wisdom, or the exertions of their own power, (a conduct to which they had ever been prone,) they were impressively taught, that their past achievements and their present condition must be acknowledged to be of the Lord. This is the instructive truth declared in that portion of the Psalm we have now read. The meaning of our text in reference to Israel as a nation doubtless was, You are mighty and exalted, but know that the strength by which you have become so powerful, God has commanded and given; and the stability of your present elevation and your lasting and increased prosperity depend on the continued presence of God with you, and the exercise of his power in your favour: therefore, while you acknowledge him in what has been done, still let your prayer be, " Strengthen, O God, that which thou hast wrought for us."

The sentiment and spirit of this interpretation we adopt and apply to ourselves as a Christian connexion; we acknowledge that all we are is of the Lord, and by the Lord, and that our continued being as a spiritual people, and all our future prosperity in the world, must be from the Lord; therefore, it behoves us, while we gratefully confess " God has commanded our strength," most fervently to pray that his " strength " may abide with us.

In discoursing further from this scripture, it is my intense desire, on this memorable occasion, to lead you to trace all that is great and good in Methodism to God. In doing so, we observe,

First. It is our duty, as Methodists, to contemplate, with gratitude to God and acknowledged dependence on him, the strength he has commanded, and the work which he has wrought among us.

Secondly. It will be our safety and our interest, as a Christian people, to manifest the fervency of our gratitude, and sincerity of our acknowledgments, by persevering prayer to God for his continued blessing. Taking this view of our subject, we proceed gratefully to acknowledge that,

1. By the strength and work of God we have received our existence and name as a Christian people. The language of St. Peter, addressed to the saints of his day, may with rigid truth and strict propriety be applied to us: " Ye are a chosen generation, a royal priesthood, a peculiar people, called out of darkness into his marvellous light: which in time past were not a people, but are now the people of God: which had not obtained mercy, but now have obtained mercy." (1 Pet. ii. 9, 10.) We were not, but now we are; we had no name among the tribes of Israel, but now we have a well-known name in the earth; and we have no hesitancy in asserting that the same mighty power that at first said, " Let there be light,

and there was light," made us to be a people. The venerable Wesley ever considered that revival of religion in this land, of which he and his coadjutors were the honoured instruments, as the special work of the "strength of God." His words are, " What is it that the Methodists have done, and are now doing? or rather, what is it that God hath done, and is still doing, in our land? For it is not the work of man which hath lately appeared. All who calmly observe it must say, ' This is the Lord's doing, and it is marvellous in our eyes.'"* On another occasion, again calling the spread of scriptural holiness in experience and practice the work of God, he observes, "It is no cant word, it means the conversion of sinners from sin to holiness."† Describing the commencement of this work, he states, " I was continually importuned to preach in one and another church, and that not only morning, afternoon, and night, on Sunday; but on week-days also. Vast multitudes flocked together; but in a short time, partly because of those unwieldy crowds, partly because of my unfashionable doctrine, I was excluded from one and another church, and, at length, shut out of all. Not daring to be silent, after a short struggle between honour and conscience, I made a virtue of necessity, and preached in the middle of Moorfields. Here were thousands upon thousands, abundantly more than any church could contain; and numbers among them who never went to any church or place of worship at all. More and more of them were cut to the heart, and came to me, all in tears, inquiring with the utmost eagerness, what they must do to be saved. I said, ' If all of you will meet on Thursday evening, I will advise you as well as I can.' The first evening twelve persons came; the next week, thirty or forty. Thus, without any previous plan or design, began the Methodist Society in England; a company of people associating together to help each other to work out their own salvation."‡ Speaking of the subjects of this work, he states, " Not a few whose sins were of the most flagrant kind, drunkards, swearers, thieves, whoremongers, and adulterers, have been brought 'from darkness unto light, and from the power of Satan unto God.' Many

---

* Works, vol. i., p. 150. † Ibid, vol. xiii., p. 294.
‡ Ibid. . vii., pp. 422, 423.

of these were rooted in their wickedness, having long gloried in their shame, perhaps for a course of many years, yea, even to hoary hairs. Many had not so much as a notional faith, being Jews, Arians, Deists, or Atheists. Nor has God only made bare his arm in behalf of open publicans and sinners; but many of the Pharisees also have believed on him, and have been made partakers of an inward vital religion; even righteousnesss, and peace, and joy in the Holy Ghost.' The manner in which God hath wrought this work in many souls is as strange as the work itself. It has generally, if not always, been wrought in one moment. ' As the lightning shining from heaven,' so was ' the coming of the Son of man,' either to bring peace or a sword; either to wound or to heal; either to convince of sin, or to give remission of sins in his blood."*

From these recorded sentiments of our esteemed Founder, it is manifest that he considered Methodism to have its origin in a divine power, and accounted it a great work, of the Lord's doing. Indeed, only a full conviction of this could have sustained him in all that he had to sacrifice, to suffer, and to do. Of the correctness of his views we think all unprejudiced persons must be sensible, if they duly consider that the principal instrument himself was led in a way that he knew not, nor even desired to know; for such was his strong and even bigoted attachment to that church of which he was an ordained Minister, that he would scarcely admit that a soul could be saved beyond her pale; and yet from her sanctuaries he was excluded, and forced to make the field his temple, and the world his parish. The change also effected in the conduct of those to whom he ministered the Gospel of salvation, could only be wrought by God; the most depraved of men became holy in all manner of conversation; the most worthless characters, valuable members of civil society; and the most miserable and wretched of human beings, comfortable in their circumstances, and truly happy. They experienced a change of that indisputable moral nature, that neither the wisdom of the wise, nor the power of the legislator, ever did or could effect. The opposition, likewise, that the work had to withstand, and the difficulties it had to encounter and surmount, were such as no human system

---

* Works, vol. i., pp. 150, 151.

could have accomplished or resisted. To this conclusion the unbiassed mind must come;—if Methodism had not been wrought of God, it would never have been established, or long since must have come to nought, and the remembrance of it would now only be found with the records of human folly. But having taken root, obtained stability, and yielded sacred fruit, we are warranted to conclude, the hand that formed us a people was divine.

2. By the strength and work of God, we possess the holy essential doctrines which form the creed of our Christian faith, and the godly discipline by which we are governed. We say not that the doctrines believed by us as a body are all exclusively methodistical, many of them are received by other Christian communities; but we do assert that they were specially given to us of God. The way in which our revered Wesley was led to a knowledge of them marks the guiding influence and holy teaching of that Spirit which leads into all truth. When he was first asked, "Does the Spirit of God bear witness with your spirit that you are a child of God?" he observes, "I was surprised, and knew not what to answer." When asked again, "Do you know Jesùs Christ?" his only answer was, "I know he is the Saviour of the world." When it was further inquired, "Do you know he has saved you?" he replied, "I hope he has died to save me."*

Such was the state of ignorance, in reference to experimental religion, in which these questions found him; notwithstanding his extensive learning, his varied reading, his previous frequent fasting, and days of prayer. But from this period, inquiry was excited, light began to dawn on his mind, and shortly after he was led to a saving knowledge of the truth as it is in Jesus, and to form correct views of the vital doctrines of Christianity. When he first began to preach those doctrines, now received by us as a system of divine truth, they were but little known: if found in certain articles of faith, they were scarcely ever named in the pulpit. They were accounted novel, and being deemed such, the pulpits of the Establishment were closed against him, though he clearly proved them to be the doctrines of the Bible and of the homilies of the Church.

---

* Works, vol. i., p. 23.

To define at large the whole of these doctrines would greatly exceed the limits of a discourse; to give a summary of those of a more prominent character and interest will be sufficient. We believe in the existence of one living and true God, who is a pure Spirit, without body, parts, or passions, self-existent, and eternal; supreme above all other beings; infinitely wise, holy, just, true, and merciful; omnipotent in power, and filling immensity with his presence. In the unity of the Godhead; that there are three persons of one substance, power, and glory; the Father, the Son, and the Holy Ghost. That the holy Scriptures contain all things necessary to salvation, and form the only authorized rule of faith and practice. That there is a just and gracious providence general to all creatures, special to mankind, and particular to God's faithful people, making all things work together for their good. That man, who came out of the hands of his Maker in a state of perfect holiness and happiness, fell from his original rectitude, became dead in sin, and is totally and universally corrupt; and that his moral defilement is transmitted to all his posterity. That the Lord Jesus Christ, the Redeemer of the world, is very God and very man, uniting in one person the Godhead and the manhood; who, by his sufferings and death, made a full and satisfactory atonement for sin, so as to satisfy the demands of divine justice, and procure not only reconciliation, but an everlasting inheritance in the kingdom of heaven. That the merit of his death is not limited, but as extensive as the depravity of man; " being made a little lower than the angels for the suffering of death, that he, by the grace of God, should taste death for every man;" he thus became " a propitiation for the sins of the whole world;" and the " Saviour of all, specially of those who believe." That man, in order to salvation, must repent of and forsake all sin, and believe in the Lord Jesus Christ with the heart unto righteousness. Such also as the doctrines of justification by faith alone in the Redeemer's atoning blood; adoption into God's favour and family, so as to cry, " Abba, Father;" the direct testimony of the Spirit of God with our spirit that we are his children; the regeneration of depraved nature by the renewing power of the Holy Spirit; thus giving an assurance of a state of salvation, and an earnest of an eternal inheritance. Further, we believe that it is the privilege of the believer to be saved from all sin, made perfect in love, and fully conformed to the image of God, through the sanctification of the Spirit. That it is possible for saints to fall from their steadfastness, " make shipwreck of faith," thus " fail of the grace of God," and finally " draw back unto perdition:" but, " abiding " in Christ, and " continuing patient in well-doing" unto the end, God will render unto them " glory, honour, immortality, and eternal life." Finally, that man will be raised from the dead, and stand before the judgment-seat of Christ, and receive according to the deeds done in the body: that the blessedness of the righteous, and the misery of the wicked, will be eternal; for the saint will ever be with the Saviour, but the sinner will be " punished with everlasting destruction from the presence of the Lord." Such are the doctrines which have been committed to us to keep; and though some of them have been disputed, *we* find them all in the Scriptures of truth, and boldly affirm that, while none of them can be proved to be pernicious to morals, or endangering to happiness, the belief of many of them is essential to salvation, and, when received in power, they are attended with holiness and happiness, and finally conduct to heaven. Now we receive these doctrines from God, and in doing so, confess he has " commanded strength unto us," even the strength of life and salvation.

Thus the charge, that Methodism is a new religion, which has only existed one hundred years, and therefore cannot be true, is as false as it is foolish. As a religious body we have only existed for that period of time, and it is in reference to this we acknowledge the apostolic Wesley to be our founder, but not the founder of those doctrines which form our religious creed. He was taught them by the word of God, where they have existed ever since that word was dictated by the Holy Spirit. Hence he never spake of Methodism in its doctrines as his work, but invariably as a revival of the religion preached by the Prophets and Apostles of the Lord. We repel, therefore, with holy jealousy for God's glory, the insinuation that Methodism in its doctrines is new: this would reduce it to a mere human system; we claim for it divine authority.

Equally we acknowledge the hand of his goodness and the

command of his power in our godly discipline, which, for simplicity, purity, and righteousness, will bear a comparison with the rules and regulations of any other Christian society. Our observations on this part of our economy must of necessity be very brief. We commence with the reception of members. Of those who seek membership with us, one plain condition is required, " a desire to flee from the wrath to come, and be saved from sin;" giving evidence of the sincerity of this desire by doing no harm, by avoiding evil of every kind, by doing good after their power, as they have opportunity, both to the bodies and the souls of men. To be continued in society with us, it is required that members should give evidence of their fervent desire of salvation, by attending upon all the ordinances of God, such as public worship, the ministry of the Gospel, the supper of the Lord, private prayer, and reading of the Scriptures, with the observance of fasting or abstinence. These, observes the father of Methodism, are the " general rules of our Societies, all of which we are taught of God to observe in his written word, the only and sufficient rule both of our faith and practice; and all these, we know, his Spirit writes on every truly awakened heart."*

In reference to the government of the Societies, in the regulation to guide the Pastor and the people, we find the same purity and equity. The Preacher, in order to give those who profess to be awakened the opportunity of obtaining good and showing their sincerity, can give them a note on trial after they have met a few times in class; but the Leaders' Meeting has a right to declare any persons on trial improper to be received into the Society, and after such declaration the Preacher cannot admit them: and no persons can be expelled from the Society by the Preacher for any breach of rules, or even for an act of immorality, till such fact or crime has been proved at a Leaders' Meeting.† We may also observe, in the appointment of officers, such as Leaders and Stewards, the nomination is with the Preacher, but the approval or rejection is with the Leaders' or the Quarterly Meetings. The same regulation is binding in reference to the admission of persons to act as Local Preachers.‡ Thus while office-bearers cannot force on the

---

* Works, vol. viii., pp. 270, 271.   † See Class Book and Large Minutes.
‡ Minutes for 1797.

Pastor any person objectionable to him, neither can he impose any one on them they may deem improper for the office to which he is nominated. We further notice, all candidates for the ministry must be approved by the Quarterly Meeting before they can be recommended to the Conference to become regular Preachers.* So that the officers of the respective Societies have a conservative power, both over the members and the ministry; the Pastor cannot act without them, and they cannot act independently of him.

In reference to Chapels, we may notice, the trust-deed secures to the Preacher appointed by the Conference the right of occupancy for a limited time, on certain terms; and the Trustees are the guardians of the Chapels to see the observance of the terms required; namely, that the Minister preaches the doctrines contained in our Founder's Notes on the New Testament, and first four volumes of sermons; possesses competent gifts for the work of the ministry; and maintains true godliness of character.† The propriety of these regulations must be manifest to every reflecting mind, and mark, we think, the direction of that wisdom which is from above; and the excellency of the whole may be summed up in the fact, that Wesleyan Methodism in doctrine and discipline cannot change; it must remain what it has been and now is: other doctrines cannot be preached, nor can our government be altered. In this we see, and joyfully admit, that "God has commanded our strength," and wrought a great and gracious work for us as a people.

3. By the strength and work of God, we have been preserved when assailed by outward persecution, or agitated by internal strife and division. If Methodism cannot name its martyrs who have been burned at the stake, yet it can tell of its numerous sufferers, who have had to endure not merely the infamy of reproach and scorn, but also violence in their persons, the destruction of their property, and imprisonment for Christ's sake; yea, even some who, in consequence of the cruel treatment they received from merciless mobs, found an early tomb. The rage of persecution in the infancy of Methodism, for fury and acts of malignant wantonness, has seldom been surpassed. The lives of the Wesleys, and the early Preachers, were fre-

---

* Minutes for 1797.   † Plan of Pacification, Minutes for 1795.

quently in jeopardy in various parts of the land, and that not always from the lowest of the people, but also from those of elevated stations in life. On the subject of persecution, the laborious Wesley has observed, " In truth, the god of this world was not asleep, neither was he idle. He did fight, and that with all his power, he brought forth all his hosts to war; he stirred up the beasts of the people, and they roared like lions." * Indeed, the common opinion was, " You may treat them as you please, for there is no law for them." But law was found even for them; the Lord put it into the heart of King George the Second to interpose in their behalf. A Magistrate called on the persecuted Wesley, and informed him " that he need not suffer the riotous mobs to molest him." " Sir," he observed, " we have orders from above to do you justice." † These days of storm and tempest have long since passed by, the persecutions of modern times have been comparatively mild and harmless, the persecution of evil words; now we have rest from violent deeds; the Lord's strength has stilled the madness of the people, and the law of the land gives us liberty and affords us protection. Even this we confess is a " work wrought for us " by the Lord, and it is marvellous in our eyes.

The interpositions of divine power in our behalf have been no less manifest in preserving us in the midst of internal tumult and disquietude. Men of changeable minds and turbulent dispositions have, at different periods of our history, endeavoured to introduce error in doctrine, and change in our discipline; and thus make us any thing but *Wesleyan Methodists;* and such have been their wiles, and wrathfulness, that we may indeed say, with ancient Israel, " If it had not been the Lord who was on our side when men rose up against us, then they had swallowed us up quick; when their wrath was kindled against us, then the waters had overwhelmed us." (Psal. cxxiv. 3.) By these commotions, our Zion has been shaken, but it has been to take deeper root and attain firmer stability: the fire has tested our principles, but has failed to consume them; faithful men have been found to withstand these modern Alexanders, and they have gone " out from us,

---

* Works, vol. vii., p. 210.   † Moore's Life of Wesley, vol. ii., p. 2.

because they were not of us; for if they had been of us, they would have continued with us;" and while some of them have now neither name nor inheritance in the church of God, we are a people " saved by the Lord." We rejoice to observe, yea, and we will rejoice, that after having endured, for one hundred years, various and violent storms from without, and fierce and flaming fires of contention from within, we were never more firmly established, never more affectionately united, never more universally peaceful, never more rich in benevolence, nor ever more prosperous, than at the present day. Surely the Lord hath been mindful of us for good, and for us has " wrought his marvellous works, his wonders, and his judgments."

4. By the strength and work of God we were empowered to form, and have been enabled, to the present, to support, the various and valuable institutions which are found among us. The influence and blessedness of Methodism in these things has excited the admiration and astonishment even of her enemies; in its institutions it has been a good to thousands of thousands, both in things temporal and spiritual. We refer not now to institutions without her pale, to which she has extended her frequent and ready aid; but to those which have had their origin in Methodism, or are solely supported by her members and friends. As one of the first in order, we notice the Benevolent, or Strangers' Friend Society. It is with pleasure we observe, that similar societies are now numerous in the land, but they began in Methodism. The first was formed in London, in the year 1785, to which the charitable Wesley was one of the earliest subscribers. In a letter to the founder, his words are, " I like the design and rules of your little Society, and hope you will do good to many. I will subscribe threepence per week, and will give you a guinea in advance, if you will call on me on Saturday morning."* Some years after, he observes, " I met the Strangers' Society, instituted, not for the relief of members of our Society, but for poor, sick, friendless strangers. I do not know that I ever heard or read of such an institution till within a few years ago. So this also is one of the fruits of Methodism."† Since that period more

---

* Account of the Strangers' Friend Society, by Dr. John Gardner, p. 24.
† Works, vol. iv., p. 481.

than one hundred thousand pounds have been raised annually, millions of poor have been relieved, and not a few rescued from abject want, and through this stream of benevolence, preserved from untimely death. As branches of this institution, we may name the various Dorcas and Lying-in Societies. We notice, secondly, Sunday Schools. The celebrated Raikes, of honourable memory, from whose meed of praise we would not detract a single note, is supposed to have originated these valuable institutions; but, though he might be the first to contemplate their wide extension, they existed in Methodism twelve years before he engaged in them.* They had, like many other things among us, a very humble beginning, but now are established in most of our Societies both at home and abroad; and we number them by thousands, and children by tens of thousands. Connected with these, we have also our Day, Infant, and Adult Schools. We may notice, thirdly, our numerous and efficient Tract Societies, our useful and prosperous Missionary Society; also, our Chapel Relief Fund, and Theological Institution for the help of young Ministers. For these purposes many thousands of pounds are contributed yearly; to which we may this year add the centenary gifts to the amount of more than two hundred thousand pounds. And yet we are not a rich people, and we have scarcely an inducement to desire to become rich; for though it is not impossible for riches and piety to be united, yet wealth, both to individuals and churches, is dangerous to spiritual prosperity. Thus it is our glory that these valuable benevolent institutions are not supported by the large subscriptions of the few, but by the small productive subscriptions of the many. It is, indeed, one of the peculiar excellencies of Methodism, that it unites almost all circumstances and all the abilities of its members in its designs, and nearly all of them, if their hearts are in right keeping, may, more or less, participate in her acts of goodness and charity. Yet we trace this benevolence to the Lord; he not only bestows this strength on his people, but he inspires them with the spirit to employ their strength to his praise, leading them with a perfect heart and willing mind to offer abundantly.

---

* Miss Ball's Life, p. 9.

5. By the strength and work of God, we have extended our borders, not only through the length and breadth of our own country, but to numerous and distant nations of the earth. When we take a survey of this wondrous work, from its commencement, and then contemplate it in its present extent and magnitude, we may indeed say, "Behold, how great a matter a little fire kindleth." When our Founder first began his labours, "small and feeble was his day." How little did he himself conceive what would be done, when, in the seclusion of Oxford, he began to read Kempis's Christian's Pattern, and Bishop Taylor's Rules of Holy Living and Dying, by which was produced in him an earnest desire to flee from the wrath to come; then he had not one with him to guide or help him.* Equally contracted were his views when he preached his first sermon in one of the smallest villages and least churches in England.† Little did he then anticipate the thought and fact, that his benevolent desires and labours could only be bounded by the extent of the world, and that open space would become the scene of his ministry. Nay, how far from his thought were the labours to which he was called, and the good he was to be the honoured instrument of effecting, when, in the ever to be remembered Whitsun-week of the year 1738, God made himself known to his servant as a pardoning God of love. But then his heart began to beat with a new impulse, and received an impetus death only could arrest; then his mighty soul was inflamed with an expansive principle; "the love of Christ constrained him;" and having "obtained mercy" he could not forbear from proclaiming in the highways of the land,

"The arms of love that compass me,
Would all mankind embrace."

Speaking of the commencement of his public labours, he observes: "Two or three Clergymen began vehemently to call sinners to repentance. Many thousands gathered together to hear them; and in every place where they came, many began to show such concern for religion as they never had done before. Many in a short time were deeply convinced of the number and heinousness of their sins, of their inability to

---

* Works, vol. vii., p. 421.   † South Leigh, Oxfordshire.

help themselves, and of the insignificancy of outside religion. And f.om this repentance sprung fruits meet for repentance; the whole form of their life was changed. Neither was this all; but, over and above this outward change, they began to experience inward religion; the love of God was shed abroad in their hearts. And this revival of religion has spread to such a degree, as neither we nor our fathers have known. There is scarce a considerable town in the kingdom where some have not been made witnesses of it. It has spread to every age and sex, to most orders and degrees of men, and even to abundance of those who, in time past, were accounted monsters of wickedness." *

Thus could he rejoice in the pleasure of the Lord prospering in his hands. And yet since those days, in reference to Methodism, we may ask, with astonishment and gratitude, " What hath God wrought in the enlargement of this great work?" The little cloud has not only spread and poured forth its fertilizing showers over the whole of our native land, but extended its influence to Europe, to America, to Asia, to Africa, to numerous isles of the sea, and even to the antipodes of our earth; so that now the sun never ceases to shine on the members of our Zion. At the period the indefatigable Wesley, full in years and rich in usefulness, left his labours on earth for his rest above, the number of Methodists amounted to one hundred and forty thousand. The solemn event of his death took place in March, 1791, and in his last moments he felt the support, the peace, and the cheering blessedness of that Gospel he had so successfully preached to others. It was his rest and his foundation. He trusted not to what he had been, nor to what he had done; Christ was his only confidence; repeating with great solemnity the words of the hymn,

" I the chief of sinners am,
But Jesus died for me."

He gloried not in the honour which had been conferred on him, to be the chosen instrument of reviving Bible religion in the land. He gloried not in the number of churches he had planted, and churches which were his praise among men. He gloried not in the sacrifices he had made, the sufferings he had

---

* Works, vol. vii., p. 425

endured, nor in his extensive and unwearied labours. He gloried not in the success of his long life of toil and usefulness: but in death he glorified his God, exclaiming with his expiring breath, " The *best* of *all* is, God is with us," and entered into the joy of his Lord. God has continued with his spiritual descendants, blessing them and making them a blessing, and greatly multiplying them in the earth; so that at the last Conference the number of members was, one million, one hundred and twelve thousand, five hundred and nineteen. Thus in one hundred years have the few and feeble become numerous and mighty; and if to the living on earth we add those who during the centenary of our existence have joined the church above, they form a glorious company, to the honour of divine grace; for in the number of our members, and extent of our borders, we acknowledge the strength of God, and confess our " God gave the increase." We take no glory to the creature; our language is, with heart-felt sincerity and gratitude, " Not unto us, O Lord, not unto us, but unto thy name give glory, for thy mercy and for thy truth's sake." (Psal. cxv. 1.)

We proceed to observe,

Secondly. It will be our safety and our interest, as a Christian people, to manifest the fervency of our gratitude, and the sincerity of our acknowledgments, by persevering prayer to God for his continued blessing.

In directing your attention to this part of our subject, we shall notice two things,—the object, and the spirit, of this prayer. The text presents for our adoption,

1. The object of this prayer. " Strengthen, O God, that which thou hast wrought for us." This request, that God will strengthen that which he has wrought for us, doubtless includes,

(1.) *Prayer for increased stability. That God would strengthen the strength he has given, and make stable the work he has wrought.*—Greatly should we err in spirit before the Lord, were we to conclude, as a people, that we are so deeply rooted and so firmly founded that we need no accession of strength. The very conclusion would manifest our weakness, and show that our confidence was not in God but in ourselves; a certain mark of shaking and decay, and a proof that prosperity was working our destruction. David, in the moment of elevation, once said, " I shall never be moved: Lord, by thy favour thou hast made my mountain to stand strong." But he was brought to confess, " Thou didst hide thy face, and I was troubled." (Psal. xxx. 7.) Observe, David acknowledged that the favour of God had made him strong, he took no glory of becoming great unto himself, the Lord had the praise; but his deceitful heart led him to suppose that having attained such strength he was secure in the possession of happiness. No wonder that the Lord was displeased, and taught him the necessity of a continued supply of strength to hold fast whereunto he had attained. Now David as an individual could not require the perpetuated help of God more than we do as a people. It is true, and we rejoice in the truth, that we have incontrovertible reasons to conclude that we are resting on the Rock of Ages; that we are not merely planted, but have hold of strength; but " if the foundations be destroyed," if the hand that formed us is withdrawn, " what can the righteous do?" We should become faint and feeble, and be overwhelmed with contempt. Let us then remember that our being, and our continued well-being, is yet with the Lord, and that he only can " establish, strengthen, and settle" that which he has wrought for us; a consideration that should prompt us with fervour to pray, " Be thou, O God of our salvation, our abiding strength."

(2.) *Prayer for constant protection, " O God, strengthen that which thou hast wrought for us, by keeping around us thine everlasting arms."*—Many have been our enemies, and many we may expect our enemies will be; numerous are the dangers from which we have been preserved, and to numerous dangers we may yet be exposed; powerful opposition has been withstood, and mighty opposition may still be presented. We have cause to know that Satan is not, and we hope never will be, satisfied with us. We are sworn foes, having for our object the subversion of his rule in the world. We may therefore be confident that he will continue to muster and marshal his hosts against us; and if they do not assail us in the boldness of open persecution, their attacks may be no less malicious and dangerous. There is a subtle serpent in the land, and we must not be surprised if he should cross our path. Already the wily serpent of Popery, charged with the deadly venom of error and corruption, has begun to hiss, and he will not be wanting in disposition to poison and destroy. Even now this foe rears a bold and daring front, and should he recover any strength of dominion, it requires little penetration to see that Methodism will have to bear the brunt of his triumph and wrath. Needful in that day (should it ever be allowed to come) will be the protecting strength of God. But in guarding against foes and dangers, our watchful attention must not be confined to assaults from without, we must also be cautious of movements and workings within; the workings of carnality, lukewarmness, worldly-mindedness, and vain-glorying; glorying in what we are, and thus ceasing to strive to become what God designs us to be. From this leaven of the mystery of iniquity danger may be feared; for we have more to dread from ourselves than from our avowed foes. If ever Methodism is destroyed, it will die a suicidal death. That we may have protection from these evils, we have need to pray, "Guard, O Lord, that which thou hast wrought for us."

(3.) *Prayer for continued and abundant prosperity. "Strengthen what thou hast wrought, that we may greatly multiply and yet widely extend."*—We cannot but rejoice in the number of our Israel, and in the extent of the inheritance with which the Lord hath "blessed us hitherto;" but he can make us yet a "greater people," and cause our present "mount to be too narrow for us." Giving glory to God for what we are, we dare to assert that comparatively we are nothing to what we may be, if faithful to our high vocation. We who form the present generation of Methodists, have seen great things, but the next, if they abide whereunto they are called, will see still greater things. If Methodism, commencing with the few, and with only one instrument, without any place of worship, or any institutions of utility, destitute of plan, suspected, despised, opposed, and persecuted, has in one hundred years attained to her present number, glory, and magnitude; what may she not be at the end of her second century, commencing it as she does with a regular organized system, with her well-tried rules and measures, with her numerous members and Ministers, with her thousands of chapels and schools, with her valuable institutions and with her various vigorous agency? Why, with the blessing of God, her hundreds may become millions, her "one lot a thousand," and she may be known to every nation and tongue, and felt in her holy influence through the whole of the human family. For what is Methodism but scriptural Christianity? and what are the designs of God by scriptural Christianity? Nothing less than the conversion of the world; the salvation of every soul of man. For this, then, we should pray, " Strengthen, O God, that which thou hast wrought for us, by enlarging the place of our tents, stretching forth the curtains of our habitation, lengthening our cords, and strengthening our stakes."

(4.) *Prayer for permanency of existence.* "*Strengthen, O God, that which thou hast wrought for us, that as a holy and useful people we may be preserved, and flourish to the end of time.*"—When Methodism first commenced, it was deemed by many to be the mere fleeting novelty of the day, which would soon be entombed in oblivion; and when its Founder was removed by death, numerous were the fears of some, and strong the desires of others, that it would come to nought. Since that period, persecuting foes, and treacherous children, have said, in the malignant spirit of extermination, "Rase it, rase it to the foundations thereof." Still Methodism lives by the strength of God, and that strength which has supported her to the present, can preserve her to the end of time, and cause her to live for ever in her glorified members. We speak of the second Centenary of Methodism, but we would set no limits to its days, persuaded, as we are, if it remains that holy, that efficient, that soul-saving system it now is, it will continue as long as sun and moon endure. Its permanency is a blessing inseparably connected with the possession of the strength of God. Without him it will wither and perish from the earth, and pass away to be known no more; but with him it will flourish with undeclining vigour. " Strengthen then, O God, that which thou hast so graciously wrought for us, that as a people we may be thy praise to all generations." Having noticed the object, we shall now

2. Consider the spirit of this prayer.

Thus we should pray, (1,) *In the spirit of humble dependence on God.*—To this we have encouragement from the gracious relation in which the Lord is pleased to stand to his church. " *Thy God* has commanded thy strength." Such he declares himself to be to all his saints; " I will be their God, saith the

Lord, and they shall be my people." Such we confess him to be: he is our God, our only God and Saviour. Being thus revealed to us, and thus claimed by us, we may pray with confident dependence on him that he will hear us and grant to us the desire of our hearts. Our God will bless us. We have encouragement also to pray with humble dependence on God from what he has done for us. The work he has wrought is a standing monument of the greatness of his power and the freeness of his grace; from it we cannot doubt either his ability or his willingness to accomplish all that may concern us, and bestow all that may be needed by us. Plead, then, for the strength of God in your behalf, as a Christian people, with all the confidence of mighty faith; and be assured they who honour him by giving glory to his power and fidelity, will be honoured by him with the manifestations of his goodness and grace.

(2.) *In the spirit of zeal and activity.*—There are many things we ask of God, which are immediately granted on our pleading, believing prayer; but there are other things which call for holy zeal and laborious exertion in order to be realized. Of this character is the object of this prayer. Would we have the strength of God for our establishment, protection, prosperity, and perpetuity; we must employ appointed means to secure the answer of prayer. We must personally adorn the doctrines of the Gospel by a holy conduct and conversation; we must earnestly contend for the faith delivered unto us; we must watch against evil, and steadfastly resist it in every form, name, and place; we must continue cheerfully, and if possible with increased liberality, to support those measures and institutions which have conducted us, through God's blessing, to our present eminence and strength; we must diligently cultivate the Lord's vineyard at home, and increase the number of ambassadors to the heathen. With these determinations we must pray, or supplication will be in vain. Prayer and practice must be united; then will the Lord appear unto us in all his glory, and upon our glory will be a defence.

(3.) *In the spirit of holy praise for what the Lord hath wrought among us as a people.*—Praise for past mercies is prevailing prayer for future blessings; and have we not cause to praise the strength of God for the personal good we have received? How did Methodism find many? It found them poor in their circumstances, low in their station in society, destitute of character, intemperate in their habits, and indolent and improvident in their conduct. And what has it done for them? It has taught them industry and economy, and has given them influence and respectability; and while its members generally have through its means been blessed in their basket and store, not a few have risen to affluence. Some few thus indebted to Methodism have ungratefully suffered their riches to become a snare to them, have withdrawn from membership with us, and sought what they have deemed more honourable company with which to journey to heaven; but many with the increase of worldly wealth have retained their primitive attachment to their early friends, and have either died among us, or yet live with us, serving their generation, and acknowledging that Methodism has been to them in things temporal a great and visible good. But to extend our inquiry to our moral condition. Methodism found many of us grossly ignorant, awfully depraved, desperately wicked, the enemies of God, the servants of Satan, most miserable, and without hope of heaven. And what has it done for us through the Gospel? It has enlightened our understanding, renewed our nature, changed our hearts, reformed our lives, led us to the knowledge of God as a pardoning God of love, possessed our minds with perfect peace and pure joy, and opened to us the enlivening prospects of eternal glory. And shall we not praise the Lord? What has it done for our families? Has it not been the means, under God, of the conversion from the error of their ways of many of our parents, our partners, our children, and various relations; so that now we have as much joy over them as formerly we had sorrow? And for their salvation shall we not praise the Lord? What has it done for our country? We do not scruple to assert that it has been, and now is, a national blessing. It found the land a dreary waste, covered with moral darkness, dreadfully wicked, almost destitute of the form of godliness, a valley of dry bones; and it has been the means of diffusing light, increasing knowledge, and spreading the life of scriptural Christianity through the length and breadth of the kingdom. What has it done for other denominations? To learn its sanctified influence on them, we need only compare their past lifeless state, when Wesley and Whitefield commenced their holy career, with their present state of vitality, energy, and holy zeal; and the contrast will prove that, both to the Establishment and dissenting churches of the land, it has been an extensive good; rousing them from their slumber, and provoking them to love and good works. And though from some of their children we may receive evil for good, we will nevertheless praise God for their increased and increasing spiritual prosperity. What has it done for the world at large? It has soothed the sorrows of the captive, and assisted to break the bonds of the oppressed; it has raised heathen tribes from the deepest depths of moral degradation and corruption into a state of spirituality and purity; it has civilized the most savage of men, changed them into beings of humanity, and led them to cultivate the habits, the comforts, and intercourse of social life; it has turned the idolater from the worship of the work of his own hands, to bow with reverence and sacred adoration before "the one only and true God." In a word, it has made the wilderness to bloom and blossom, the desert to rejoice and be glad, and the rocks and mountains of the solitary places of the earth to resound with hallelujahs to the Lord. Then when we bow the knee in prayer to God, our lips should also show forth his praise for the mighty works he hath done. In this spirit of confidence, of zeal, of fervent gratitude, let your language be, "Strengthen, O God, that which thou hast wrought for us."

In conclusion, permit me, as one of your Pastors, and as one who has some knowledge of the value and advantages of Methodism, having been a member nearly one half its past centenary, and one of its Ministers bordering on forty years, permit me, I say, with fervent love for your best interests, and the interests of that world of which I cannot expect many years longer to be an inhabitant, to address you.

Methodists, and especially the younger members of society, be faithful to your God, and be faithful to yourselves. Your fathers are not, they rest with their Lord; and you have entered into the fruit of their sufferings and their labours. Your elder brethren are also passing away, but they leave with you a solemn, important, and valuable trust:—Methodism, pure in its doctrines, godly in its discipline, mighty in its strength, vigorous in its operations, benevolent in its spirit, glorious in its success, embracing the world in its designs of mercy, and as a host for multitude. Hold fast faithfully, fully, and perseveringly, that good thing which we commit unto you from the Lord. Hold it fast in its scriptural faith and practice. Hold it fast in its spirit and principles. Hold it fast in its settled rules and usages. Hold it fast in its power, its fruitfulness, and in all its vitality. Hold it fast for the holy purposes for which God has commanded strength unto it,—the salvation of men, and the good of the world at large. Let it go down to your descendants, a living, working, spotless, sacred system, having written upon it, "HOLINESS UNTO THE LORD." In order to this, "stand fast in one spirit, with one mind, striving together for the faith of the Gospel; and in nothing terrified by your adversaries." To this your duty we beseech you, in the name of the Lord Jesus Christ, and solemnly charge you as those who must give an account unto God for that deposit with which you are entrusted. Thus giving full proof of fidelity, thy God, O Methodism, will continue to command thy strength, and in blessing will bless thee, and in multiplying will multiply thy seed as the stars of heaven, and as the sand upon the sea-shore;" yea, "there shall be showers of blessings" upon thee.

And now, O Lord God of heaven and earth, the God of our fathers, and our God; thou art worthy to be praised, and to be had in everlasting remembrance. Standing as we do before thee this day, at the close of one and at the commencement of another centenary of our being, as thy people, we bless thee for the wonders thou hast wrought among us, and by us; and ascribe to thee, with a ready mind, all glory, all honour, and dominion. We beseech thee to continue to command our strength, and to strengthen that thou hast wrought for us from generation to generation. Keep, we entreat thee, thy people holy, humble, zealous, and faithful; making them strong for thyself, and an increasing blessing in the world. To thee we commit them, and thy sacred cause among them. Preserve them and that cause by thy mighty power, unerring wisdom, and Holy Spirit. Clothe thou their Ministers with salvation, and make them thy chosen abiding resting place, that thy saints may ever rejoice in thy goodness; even so, Lord Jesus. Amen.

METRICAL MUSINGS
ON CENTENARY SUBJECTS.

God of our Zion, thee we praise,
To thee our hallelujahs raise,
   For wonders thou for us hast wrought:
By thee a people we are made,
In whom thou hast thy power display'd;
   A people by thy Spirit taught.

Deep sunk in sin, depraved, and blind,
Enslaved by the carnal mind,
   Were our forefathers guilty found;
No guides to teach, nor shepherd's care,
That they should to thy house repair;
   Thy laws they spurn'd, thy fear disown'd.

No warning voice to them made known
The terrors of Jehovah's frown,
   And curses which to guilt belong:
By them, the claims of heaven denied,
Transgressions great were multiplied,
   A thoughtless and ungodly throng.

Dwelling in nature's gloomy night,
Led captive by satanic might,
   Having no hope, and without God,
They wander'd wide in error's maze,
Revell'd in folly's reckless ways,
   And rapid ran sin's downward road.

On things divine they never thought,
In worldly mirth they only sought
   Desired pleasure, peace, and joy;
The promised bliss they never knew,
In vain did they its lures pursue,
   In vain the means of sense employ.

Unknown to them were prayer and praise,
Unknown were holy sabbath-days,
  And scarcely known revealed word;
Unknown were true and pure delights,
Unknown the strong, the sacred rights
  Of reason, grace, their souls, their Lord.

But glory, praise, and majesty,
Be, Lord, ascribed unto thee,
  Who didst regard their wretchedness;
Their erring hearts and lives reclaim'd,
And of such stones our Zion named,
  The nation and the world to bless.

We were not, but thou didst command
Thy servants to go through the land,
  By faith salvation to proclaim;
Freely proclaim, through Christ alone,
The world's High Priest, who did atone
  For sins of foulest deed and name.

The WESLEYS heard the voice divine,
Promptly replied, " Lord, we are thine,
  Ready thy pleasure to fulfil:
Ease, gain, and earthly honours leave,
Joyful the scorn of men receive,
  To serve thy gracious, sacred will.

" Ready to go, at thy command,
To rich and poor, throughout the land,
  And warn them from thy wrath to flee;
Ready to suffer toil or pain,
Regardless of the world's disdain,
  Our lives we freely offer thee."

Vessels prepared of the Lord,
Wise in the wisdom of his word,
  Themselves through Christ forgiven;
The Saviour they had sought and found,
His name above all names they own'd,
  For pardon, life, and hope of heaven.

Commission'd from the courts above,
Inspired with fervent, flaming love,
  True love to man, pure love to God;
Strong in the strength and might of grace,
Fraught with the truths of righteousness,
  They gladly spread themselves abroad.

Excluded from those temples where
They so delighted to appear,
  For frequent, solemn, sincere prayer;
The world their parish then became,
The universe their temple's name,
  And vile outcasts of men their care.

For these they wander'd far and wide,
To these they preach'd the Crucified,
  And dared the ruthless, mocking throng;
For these they want, fatigue, endured,
To infamy became inured,
  The theme and sport of carnal song.

For these their lives they valued not,
Fame, friends, and home, and self forgot,
  That Christ through them might be adored;
For this they counted gain but loss,
For this they shunn'd no shame, no cross;
  True servants of their loving Lord.

Like him, the lost they kindly sought,
Like him their embassy was fraught
  With gifts, the price of precious blood;
Like him, with holy zeal they burn'd,
Blessing for cursing they return'd,
  For wrath and evil render'd good.

Nor did they pray or preach in vain,
Many were by the Spirit slain,
  Confessed, mourned, and obey'd;
Wept o'er their sins with heart sincere,
Forsook those sins with godly fear,
  And fervently for mercy pray'd.

To these the messengers of peace
Offer'd a present, full release
   From grief, and guilt's oppressive load:
They told of Him, who pardon gave,
Of Him who waited all to save,
   The all-atoning Lamb of God.

The mourners, cheer'd with love's design,
With confidence and trust divine,
   On Christ believingly relied;
Sadness and sorrow fled away,
Their gloom gave place to light of day,
   With joy they " Abba, Father," cried.

Under his smile, they lived on earth,
The holy life of second birth,
   The Spirit's birth to righteousness:
Supported by that smile in death,
They praised him with expiring breath,
   And shouted " Victory " through grace.

As clouds of nature's sable night
Disperse before the morning's light,
   And day shines forth with splendour clear;
Revealing to observant eye
What vision veil'd could not descry,
   However true, however near:

So mists of gloom and error fled,
Before the beams the Gospel shed
   On Britain's late benighted isle;
Benighted with the densest cloud
That could the human mind beshroud,
   Deceive, bewilder, or defile.

Darkness of sin's destructive reign,
Which had its countless thousands slain,
  And held in dread captivity
All ranks, all ages of the land;
But now, at God's benign command,
  The Gospel came to set them free.

True moral sun, a gift divine,
It rose to quicken and to shine,
  And life, and bliss of heaven bestow;
The WESLEYS hailed its genial rays,
Received with joy those Gospel days
  The world again was called to know.

Themselves illumined with its light,
They shone around in lustre bright,
  Reflecting Gospel truth and grace;
They own'd its power, and spread its flame,
And thousands to its rising came,
  And glory saw in Jesu's face.

Long they on earth rejoiced to see
Its glad, efficient ministry;
  Its saving and renewing power:
Then, rich in fruit, and full of years,
With joy unmix'd with sighing tears,
  It cheer'd them in life's final hour.

They rested on foundation laid,
On Christ alone their souls they stay'd,
  Him Master, Saviour, they could call:
Ceasing from trust in self they cried,
" Though chief of sinners, Christ hath died,
  And he to us is all in all."

Their God was with them, God of love,
With them to take to courts above,
  With them to give prepared crown;
With them to make his promise sure,
That all who to the end endure
  " Shall with me, on my throne, sit down."

Thus Charles, in "feebleness extreme,"
Found Jesus " mighty to redeem,"
   Redeem, and grant what he desired;
A "smile from heaven," an "easy death,"
Pronouncing, with departing breath,
   " My God;" and then in peace expired.

John also could in death attest,
" He giveth to his servants rest,"
   (Happy to die and prove it thus:)
The dying saint then "Jesus" named;
" I'll praise, I'll praise," with joy exclaim'd,
   " The best of all is, God with us."

He then, without " a lingering groan,"
Committed unto God his own,
   His spirit, ransomed with blood,
In triumph enter'd into rest,
And, number'd with the countless blest,
   Before the throne of glory stood.

Welcomed with Jesus to abide,
Welcomed by all the glorified,
   Welcomed angelic joys to share;
To him as bright a crown was given,
Received by any saint in heaven,
   Who have of late been welcomed there.

Departed saint, now with thy God,
Resting from toil, to that abode
   In bands thy children follow thee:
Thousands who are to thee unknown,
Are on their way to gem that crown,
   And swell the song of victory.

Dwelling where God his own receives;
The workmen dead, the work yet lives,
   Yet lives and prospers far and wide;
Constraining us with joy to raise
This Ebenezer to his praise,
   " Their God with us doth still reside."

His sacred presence we confess,
To this ascribe that great success
   We as his honour'd people know :
The Lord indeed his arm hath bared;
At home, abroad, he has declared
   How free his mercy to bestow.

The few are greatly multiplied,
The weak have been with strength supplied,
   Assail'd, they now protection have :
Though once despised, yet now revered,
God hath in their defence appear'd,
   A mighty God, to bless and save.

From Britain's favoured isle have spread,
To lands afar, where captive led
   By Satan's wiles, adoring stood
Immortal men, who homage paid
To gods (which their own hands had made)
   With sacrifice of human blood.

To lands of death and dreary night,
Where God of life and God of light
   Received no fear, and had no name:
But lands where now his name is known,
And men his holy worship own,
   And him their pard'ning Father claim.

The slave the Gospel has made free,
The savage raised to dignity,
   And idol worshippers has taught
To hate, renounce their cruel creeds,
Deplore, forsake those ruthless deeds,
   With crime, with guilt, with misery fraught.

Thus hath the Lord his people blest,
And blessing made, from east to west,
   From north to south, from sea to sea :
From countless tongues new songs arise,
A burst of praise, true sacrifice,
   Of glory to God's majesty.

Head of the church, triumphant King,
The hosts above thy conquests sing,
   The saints on earth thy claims confess:
We mingle with them fervent praise,
Gladly our hearts and voices raise,
   Thy rule to celebrate and bless.

Adoring thee, for wonders wrought,
For myriads whom thy word hath taught
   To fly to Christ for saving grace:
We pray thy word yet wider still
May spread, and thy blest sacred will
   Be known in every clime and place.

Go forth in thy great strength, O Lord,
Gird on thy thigh thy conquering sword,
   Display thy mercy and thy power:
In plenitude of love appear,
Make known that love both far and near,
   On all, on all, thy Spirit shower.

The careless rouse from deadly sleep,
Constrain with godly tears to weep,
   And yield themselves entirely thine:
The formalists awake, awake,
Out of their awful slumber shake,
   And breathe in them the life divine.

Backsliders from their faithless fall,
And sinful wanderings recall;
   Upon them look once more in love:
Hear when they healing help implore,
Them to lost blessedness restore,
   And let them mercy freely prove.

Add them unto thy church again,
Henceforth may they their faith maintain,
   And steadfast in thy love abide:
In them make known thy richest grace,
Through them proclaim thy righteousness;
   In life, in death, be glorified.

And those who long have halting stood,
Between the world and living God,
  O may they with decision own,
" The Lord, the Lord, is only King,"
To God a cheerful service bring,
  To him, and him alone, bow down.

Thy faithful ones, O God, inspire
With strong, renew'd, intense desire
  Thy glory zealously to spread:
Work in them all thy sovereign will,
Their souls with thy blest fulness fill,
  The Spirit of their heavenly Head.

Their gifts of righteousness increase,
Their faith, their fear, their perfect peace,
  Their holy joy, and burning love,
Their meekness, patience, purity;
With all the mind that was in thee,
  Baptize them fully from above.

In every sacred grace to grow,
Abound in all the works which show
  To thee they consecrate their days;
With all that's lovely, Lord, endue,
Of good report, and just, and true,
  Honest and pure, commanding praise,

Thus may thy people call thee " Lord,"
In holy deed as well as word,
  Thee only for their Master own:
In acts of mercy have delight,
In fruits well-pleasing in thy sight,
  Daily their conduct constant crown.

Thy perfect life in theirs maintain,
The Christian's character sustain,
  In every circumstance and place:
Thus live the glory of thy name,
And by their tongues and lives proclaim,
  The triumphs, honours of thy grace.

And when thou dost so greatly bless
The people, saved by thy grace,
　　Their Ministers anew inspire;
Cheer with the presence of their Head,
Thy Spirit on them richly shed,
　　Spirit of power and heavenly fire.

As vessels chosen of the Lord
To bear the treasures of his word,
　　Them with the purest gifts endue;
A wise and sound discerning mind,
Knowledge with fervency combined;
　　With tender charity imbue.

With yearning pity, anxious care,
To rescue from the tempter's snare
　　All in sin's abject bondage found;
Warning the wicked of their way,
The saint to watch, believe, obey;
　　The Gospel trumpet clearly sound.

Whether men will hear or forbear,
Thy counsel uncorrupt declare,
　　To each required portion give:
To high, to low, to rich, to poor,
The young, the old, all ranks implore
　　To turn from sin to God, and live.

Not only in the world at large,
But well their mission to discharge
　　On those who in thy courts abide;
Entreat, rebuke, with mercy charm,
Or give the solemn, dread alarm,
　　And rightly word of truth divide.

As watchmen, faithful to their trust;
As stewards, true, upright, and just;
　　As shepherds, tender, kind, and wise;
As pastors, vigilant, sincere,
Not counting life itself too dear,
　　To serve thy church a sacrifice.

Thus clothed with might, with strength divine,
With every grace, O Lord, of thine,
  Again anoint, endue, and seal
Their tongues, their hearts, with holy fire,
And with thy Spirit all inspire,
  Thy deathless love, thy quenchless zeal.

Pastors and people firm unite,
To seek and to secure thy right,
  Thy peaceful kingdom to extend;
Till all shall own thy sovereign sway,
Till all thy sacred laws obey,
  And all before thy sceptre bend.

Hasten, O Lord, that day of grace,
When all shall thy mild rule confess,
  And perfect righteousness attain:
Subvert, destroy the rule of sin,
Conquer, subdue, proclaim, begin
  Thy universal endless reign.

JOYS OF A HUNDRED YEARS.

Rejoice! rejoice! hosannahs raise,
  In glory God with us appears:
Rejoice! rejoice! with songs of praise
  Hail, hail, the second hundred years.

Rejoice! rejoice! let all adore
  The Lord most high, him honour give:
Rejoice! rejoice! his grace implore,
  For greater things in him believe.

Rejoice! rejoice! loud make it known,
  What you have seen, what God has done:
Rejoice! rejoice! and praising own,
  The Lord alone the work begun.

Rejoice! rejoice! your children tell,
   The wonders God for us has wrought;
Teach them the song of praise to swell,
   Themselves from nature's bondage brought.

Teach them your Saviour's grace to show,
   Your name to bear, your faith confess;
That children yet unborn may know
   Our God, and our Redeemer bless.

Rejoice! rejoice! by faith to see
   Unnumber'd multitudes arise,
In clouds unto our Zion flee,
   And offer there pure sacrifice.

Rejoice! rejoice! the day will come
   When Christ in every land shall save;
Where sin is found, where man doth roam,
   The Gospel shall its conquests have.

Rejoice! rejoice! again rejoice,
   The glory of the Lord appears;
And hail, with one united voice,
   Joys of the second hundred years.

OUR SECOND CENTENARY.

God of our fathers, and our God,
   Thy lasting presence we implore,
Make us thy constant fix'd abode,
   Thy temple, to depart no more:
Hear us, O Lord, we thee address,
Our second Centenary bless.

For this our hearts to thee we raise,
   For this in faith we pleading pray,
Through us show forth thy name and praise,
   In us thy mind and will display;
With all the gifts of righteousness,
Our second Centenary bless.

Our works of faith and love increase,
  In bonds of charity unite,
Inflame our zeal, preserve our peace,
  From age to age direct aright:
With richest fruits of holiness,
Our second Centenary bless.

Thy house of glory glorify,
  Her courts abundantly enlarge;
And more than ever multiply
  Her watchmen, faithful to their charge:
Their word attend, and with success
Our second Centenary bless.

Ten thousand-fold increase us, Lord,
  More copiously thy Spirit shower,
Through us yet wider spread thy word,
  More gloriously display thy power;
Our second Centenary crown
Far, far, beyond what we have known.

Give our descendants, Lord, to see
  Our father's Zion and our love,
In all that pure prosperity
  Which God with them will fully prove:
In triumphs we cannot relate,
Their Centenary celebrate.

ROCHE, PRINTER, 70, OLD-STREET ROAD, LONDON.

Printed by Libri Plureos GmbH in Hamburg, Germany